KW-345-016

Acknowledgements

Barnaby's Picture Library 6 inset, 44; S. C. Bisserot 25, 32, 32 inset; J. Allan Cash 15 inset; Bruce Coleman 35, Jen and Des Bartlett back cover, 43, S. C. Bisserot 9 top, Jane Burton 28, 29 top, 33 bottom, Gerald Cubitt 18–19, 45, Francisco Erize 20, Jeff Foott 39, Dennis Green 36 bottom, P. A. Hinchcliffe 17, Udo Hirsch 33 top, Leonard Lee Rue front endpapers, 14 top, Norman Lightfoot 42, John Markham 12, Norman Myers 18, Oxford Scientific Films 26–27, J. Pearson 38, Hans Reinhard front cover, 4 bottom, 10 inset, 10–11, 11 top right, 13, 16, 22 bottom, 23, back endpapers, Simon Trevor 5, 8, John Wallis 7 bottom, Adrian Davies 29 bottom, Brian Hawkes 15, David Hosking 34, Eric Hosking 31 top, Peter Loughran 27, Natural History Photographic Agency: Douglas Baglin 6, 7 top, Anthony Bannister 9 bottom, 30 bottom, James Carmichael 30 top, E. A. Janes 24–25, Peter Johnson 36 top, Walter Murray 14 bottom; Natural Sciences Photos: C. Banks 31 bottom, Geoffrey Kinns 21, 37; Spectrum Colour Library: 4 top, 11 bottom right; Tony Stone Associates: 22 top, 40, 41.

Other books in the series:
Nature
People of the World
Things that Move

Published 1979 by
The Hamlyn Publishing Group Limited
London · New York · Sydney · Toronto
Astronaut House, Feltham, Middlesex, England

ISBN 0 600 36324 4

Printed and bound by Group Poligrafici Calderara, Bologna, Italy -

Hamlyn First Colour Books

Young Animals

Hamlyn
London · New York · Sydney · Toronto

Some baby animals are very small.
A baby kangaroo is only three centimetres long.
After six months a koala travels on his mother's back.
Kangaroos travel in the pouch until they are quite big.

Some baby animals are very big.
A baby elephant can weigh 113 kilograms.
When he grows up he may weigh over 6 tonnes.
This young rhinoceros will grow two horns.
The horns are really made of tightly pressed hair.
Baby warthogs soon grow two fierce tusks.
Can you see what these warthogs are doing?

Puppies and kittens are
born blind but their eyes
soon open.
They are helpless when
they are very young.
These young animals
are fun to play with.
They are born with soft
fur.
Do you think they look
friendlier than the
warthogs?

Mice and rabbits are born without fur.
These young dormice have only just been born.
Their mother must keep them warm.
They will soon grow a fur coat like these young
rabbits have done.
What colour are the rabbits' coats?
Would you like to have a fur coat?

Hedgehogs grow spines
instead of fur.
The spines protect them
from an enemy.
Animals live in lots of
different places.
This red squirrel lives in a
nest in the tree.
Baby foxes are born in
an underground
home called an earth.

This badger's home is underground.
It is called a set.
His bed is lined with dried grass and straw.
Wild boars are born in a warm den.
They are born with their eyes open and can stand
straight away.
They all have a stripy coat.

Zebras and giraffes are
not helpless when they
are born.
They must be able to
keep up with their
mothers when they are
running.
A zebra has stripes and
a giraffe has large spots.
These markings help the
animals to hide.
Do you remember
another young animal
with stripes?

Some animals have only one baby at a time.
This alpaca has one baby.
Do you think he is trying to hide behind his mother?
He will grow a long woolly coat called a fleece.
A young bison is called a calf.
Here is a mother bison with her baby.
They live with lots of other bison in a herd.

Donkeys and cattle usually have only one baby.
This calf is on his own.
He must learn to understand the other cattle.
His mother might be calling him.
This pig has more than one baby.
How many can you see?

A guinea pig is not
really a pig.
Do you think it looks
like one?
This guinea pig has
three babies.
They all have soft
fur with pretty
markings.
A polecat has lots of
babies at one time.
Here is a mother
polecat caring for
her young.
Can you count how
many she has to
look after?

Have you ever seen so
many spiders?
These young spiders
have just hatched from
their eggs.
Some young animals
look completely different
when they are grown up.
This caterpillar will go
to sleep and change
into a butterfly.
Would you like to wake
up one day to find
that you have wings?

A young frog changes as it grows up too.
It hatches underwater as a tadpole.
This tadpole has grown some legs.
When he is a full-grown frog he will leave the
water and live for most of the time on land.
Can you see the full-grown frog here?

All these animals hatch
from eggs.
This young alligator has
strayed from his family.
Can you see the snakes
hatching?
Here is an adder with a
baby.
Do you think these funny
lizards can see their
mother?
Can you find her against
the stone?

Some animals live for a
very long time.
Giant tortoises live for
over 100 years.
There are some small
tortoises here too.
When these chameleons
grow up they will be
able to change colour.
Sometimes they may
want to be green.

All sorts of birds hatch from eggs too.
This chick has just hatched out of his shell.
He had to make a hole in the shell with his beak.
The baby thrushes look very hungry.
Their mother has found something that they
would like to eat.
Can you see what she has in her beak?

This barn-owl has
a shrew for the babies.
They still have their first
feathers.
These cygnets are
returning from a swim.
Swans protect their
babies fiercely.
Mother and father
penguin take it in turns
to look after their young.

Male lions and bears are very lazy.
Only the females look after the cubs.
The cubs stay with their mothers until they are
grown up.
This young lion cub looks quite gentle.
He will grow up to be very fierce though.
When he is about two years old he will be able to
hunt on his own.

Some animals only stay with their mothers for a short time.
Sheep and goats grow up quickly and can leave their mothers quite soon.
Sheep and goats are closely related.
Can you see the difference between them?

Young animals are taught different things when they are born.
This young seal must know how to swim.
One of the first lessons a young beaver must learn is how to build a dam across the river.
He has sharp teeth for gnawing wood for the dam.

Here is a young monkey learning how to swing from tree to tree.
Monkeys are very good at climbing trees.
They hold on with their feet and hands and sometimes with their tails as well.
How is this monkey holding on?
This other monkey is having his fur cleaned.
Do you think he is safe on that branch?

Which young animal did you like best?
Would you like to live as he does?